E-COMMERCE 101

Everything you need to know

Philipp Frühwirth

CONTENTS

INTRODUCTION TO E-COMMERCE

E-commerce, also known as electronic commerce, has revolutionized the way people buy and sell products and services. The growth of the internet and digital technologies has brought about a new era of business, where transactions are completed using electronic communication rather than face-to-face interactions.

The concept of e-commerce is simple – it refers to the buying and selling of goods and services online. This process can occur on various platforms, including mobile devices, social media, and e-marketplaces, making it more convenient for consumers and businesses alike.

E-commerce has become increasingly popular due to its many advantages over traditional retailing. First and foremost, it eliminates geographical boundaries, allowing businesses to reach customers from all over the world. It is also faster and more efficient, reducing the time and cost associated with physical distribution. Moreover, it provides a personalized shopping experience and real-time customer support, enhancing customer satisfaction and loyalty.

There are different types of e-commerce models, including business-to-business (B2B), business-to-consumer (B2C), consumer-to-consumer (C2C), and consumer-to-business (C2B). B2B e-commerce involves the exchange of goods and services between businesses, while B2C e-commerce refers to the selling of products and services to individual consumers. C2C e-commerce involves transactions between two individuals, while C2B e-commerce allows individuals to sell their products and services to businesses.

As e-commerce continues to grow, it has become important for businesses to choose the right e-commerce platform that meets their specific needs. Popular e-commerce platforms include Shopify, Magento, WooCommerce, and BigCommerce, each offering unique features and benefits to businesses.

However, just like any other business, e-commerce businesses must comply with certain laws and regulations, including data protection, privacy, and consumer protection legislation. It is important for businesses to understand and adhere to these guidelines to avoid legal disputes and protect their reputation.

In conclusion, e-commerce has transformed the way businesses operate, offering unprecedented growth opportunities and convenience to both consumers and businesses. However, to be successful in the e-commerce world, businesses must understand the market, choose the right platform, comply with laws and regulations, and employ effective marketing strategies to attract and retain customers.

DIFFERENT TYPES OF E-COMMERCE MODELS

E-Commerce is transforming the retail industry by providing consumers with a convenient solution to shop online without any geographical or time constraints. Businesses can also benefit from e-commerce by gaining access to a global customer base.

There are several types of E-Commerce models, including the following:

1. Business-to-consumer (B2C): B2C is the most popular E-Commerce model, where businesses sell their products or services directly to consumers online. This model involves a straightforward transaction process where a customer places an order, and the business ships the product or delivers the service.

2. Business-to-business (B2B): This type of E-Commerce involves businesses selling their products or services to other businesses. In B2B, the purchasing process is often more complex than in B2C transactions as it involves higher volumes of products and services.

3. Consumer-to-consumer (C2C): C2C E-Commerce allows consumers to sell products or services to other consumers. Common examples of C2C E-Commerce include online classifieds, auctions, and peer-to-peer marketplaces.

4. Consumer-to-business (C2B): In this model, consumers offer products and services to businesses. Crowdfunding sites like Kickstarter and Patreon are examples of C2B E-Commerce platforms.

5. Business-to-government (B2G): B2G E-Commerce refers to

businesses that offer products and services to government organizations.

6. Government-to-consumer (G2C): This model involves government organizations such as the DMV selling products or services to consumers, such as driver's licenses or permits.

7. Mobile commerce (m-commerce): M-commerce involves E-Commerce transactions conducted on mobile devices. This model is gaining popularity due to the widespread use of smartphones and tablets.

8. Social commerce: Social commerce refers to E-Commerce transactions that occur through social media platforms. This model uses social media interactions and user-generated content to facilitate transactions.

Each E-Commerce model has its unique features, advantages, and disadvantages. Choosing the right model depends on the nature of the business, target audience, and the products or services being offered. By understanding each model, businesses can make informed decisions and develop strategies for success in the online marketplace.

BENEFITS OF CHOOSING E-COMMERCE OVER TRADITIONAL RETAILING

In the digital age, e-commerce has become a popular way for businesses and consumers to buy and sell goods and services online. While traditional retailing has been around for centuries, more and more businesses are choosing e-commerce due to the many benefits it offers. Here are some of the top benefits of choosing e-commerce over traditional retailing:

1. Low overhead costs: E-commerce eliminates the need for a physical storefront, which can save businesses a significant amount of money on rent, utilities, and other operational expenses. This allows businesses to offer lower prices to their customers while still maintaining profitability.

2. 24/7 availability: Unlike traditional retail stores, e-commerce websites are always open. This means customers can browse and purchase products at any time of the day, even outside of regular business hours. This increased availability can lead to a higher volume of sales and increased profits for businesses.

3. Wider customer reach: E-commerce allows businesses to reach customers from anywhere in the world, expanding their customer base beyond their local area. This can lead to increased brand awareness and recognition, as well as more sales opportunities.

4. Personalized shopping experiences: With the help of data analytics and advanced technology, e-commerce businesses can track and analyze each customer's shopping behavior and preferences. This allows businesses to personalize the shopping experience and offer targeted promotions and recommendations

that are more likely to convert into sales.

5. Lower marketing costs: E-commerce businesses can reach a wider audience at a lower cost through digital marketing strategies such as social media advertising, email marketing, and search engine optimization. This can lead to higher ROI and more effective marketing results.

6. Efficient inventory management: E-commerce businesses can track inventory levels and automatically restock products when they run low. This eliminates the need for manual tracking and reduces the risk of product shortages, ensuring that customers always have access to the products they want.

Overall, e-commerce offers significant benefits to businesses that choose to embrace it. From low overhead costs and wider customer reach to personalized shopping experiences and efficient inventory management, there are many reasons why e-commerce is the way of the future for retail businesses.

UNDERSTANDING THE E-COMMERCE MARKET AND ITS POTENTIAL

E-commerce has transformed the way businesses operate and emerge. It has disrupted traditional business models and offered a cost-efficient alternative with almost endless growth opportunities. Understanding the current state of the e-commerce market and its potential is crucial for businesses to establish themselves and make meaningful contributions.

The global e-commerce market has been growing at an amazing pace over the past decade. In 2021, the market size is predicted to reach 4.9 trillion dollars, according to Statista. This is a significant increase from 2.3 trillion dollars in 2017. As internet penetration rates continue to rise, and with advancements in technology, the market's growth is expected to continue at a comparable rate in the next few years.

Several industries have benefitted from the growth of e-commerce. They include fashion, consumer electronics, health and beauty, and household goods. According to a report by Shopify, the top-selling product categories in the United States in 2020 were fashion and beauty products, followed by home and garden, electronics, sports, and recreation equipment.

E-commerce offers a cost-efficient solution for businesses that traditionally operated offline. Online-based businesses entail lower overhead costs, such as office rent fees and utility costs. This offers small and medium-sized businesses an opportunity to compete with maestro brands without breaking the bank or sacrificing quality.

E-commerce also offers a greater potential for capturing a wider market. For example, traditional retail stores have geographical limitations that can be overcome by establishing an online business. Customers from all corners of the globe can find businesses online; hence, internationalization and accessing diverse demographics is a more comfortable and streamlined process.

Additionally, e-commerce businesses can leverage the several new sales channels, such as social media, which plays a pivotal role in growing online business sales volume. Social media, such as Instagram and Facebook, among others, are creating new opportunities for businesses to interact with their customers and target them based on their interests and preferences, enhancing customer engagement.

In conclusion, the e-commerce market offers a dynamic environment that exposes businesses to limitless opportunities. Understanding the current state of the e-commerce market and recognizing the potential it offers can assist businesses to innovate and find new ways to grow their operations. Developments in technology and changing consumer behavior will continue to drive the growth of e-commerce, making it necessary for businesses to establish an online presence to reap the benefits the industry offers.

LEGAL COMPLIANCE AND REGULATIONS FOR E-COMMERCE BUSINESSES

As E-Commerce businesses continue to grow and innovate, it has become increasingly important to understand the legal compliance and regulations surrounding online transactions. A solid understanding of the legal landscape is essential for any E-Commerce business looking to remain compliant, avoid costly fines, and protect their customers' and own financial safety. In this chapter, we will discuss the most important legal aspects of E-Commerce businesses and what you need to know to stay within the law.

One of the most essential aspects of E-Commerce compliance is data protection. If your business collects any data in the course of online transactions, you'll need to comply with relevant data protection laws, such as the General Data Protection Regulation (GDPR) in the EU or the California Consumer Privacy Act (CCPA) in the US. These regulations require businesses to obtain clear consent from customers before collecting any data, manage that data responsibly, and ensure that customers can access, rectify or delete their data at any time.

Payment card industry (PCI) compliance is another crucial consideration for E-Commerce businesses. PCI compliance helps ensure the security of credit card information and payments. The standards are issued by the Payment Card Industry Security Standards Council and apply to all businesses that accept credit cards as a form of payment. Compliance involves implementing stringent security protocols, regular monitoring, and annual testing to ensure the protection of financial data.

In addition to these regulations, E-Commerce businesses also need to comply with a variety of other laws and regulations, depending on the country or region where they operate. These include regulations related to shipping, export controls, consumer protection, and intellectual property.

It is also essential to consider the legal implications of your company's terms and conditions, privacy policy, and any other agreements you may have with customers, suppliers, or partners. These agreements should be well-drafted and clearly written to ensure that all parties understand and agree to the terms.

Finally, another crucial aspect of E-Commerce compliance is handling international transactions. Different countries have different legal requirements and regulations that can complicate cross-border transactions. International businesses must be aware of regulations related to taxes, customs duties, shipping, and international agreements.

In conclusion, compliance with regulations is an essential aspect of E-Commerce. Make sure you understand and comply with relevant data protection, PCI, and other legal frameworks. Creating well-drafted policies and agreements is equally essential. With proper legal considerations in place, you help to protect both yourself and your customers.

BUILDING AN E-COMMERCE WEBSITE FROM SCRATCH

In today's digital age, having an e-commerce website is essential for any business that wants to succeed. An e-commerce website can help you expand your reach and sell your products around the clock without any geographic limitations. Building an e-commerce website from scratch may seem like a daunting task, but the good news is that it's easier than ever before. Here are the essential steps to follow:

1. Choose a Domain Name and Hosting Provider: Your domain name is the address that people use to reach your website, and hosting is where your website data is stored. Choose a domain name that is easy to remember and relates to your business. For hosting, choose a reliable provider that offers good speed, uptime, and customer support.

2. Select an E-Commerce Platform: Selecting the right e-commerce platform is crucial for your website's success. Popular e-commerce platforms include Shopify, WooCommerce, Magento, BigCommerce, and Squarespace. You can also opt for a custom-built website, but this may be more expensive.

3. Choose a Theme and Design Your Website: Once you've selected an e-commerce platform, it's time to choose a theme and design your website. Choose a theme that fits your brand's style and offers good functionality. Ensure that your website is easy to navigate, offers an excellent user experience, and is mobile-responsive.

4. Add Products and Payment Gateways: Adding products to your e-commerce website is the most crucial step. Ensure that your

product descriptions are clear and well-defined, including high-quality images. You'll also need to integrate payment gateways such as PayPal, Stripe, or Square to facilitate transactions.

5. Install Essential Plugins: Install essential plugins such as security plugins, SEO plugins, and social media plugins to enhance your website's functionality and performance.

6. Test Your Website: Test your website to ensure it's fast, easy to navigate, and functions correctly. Ensure that all links and buttons work correctly, the shopping cart works without any glitches, and the website displays correctly on different devices.

7. Launch Your Website: Once you've tested your website, it's time to launch it. Ensure that your website adheres to all legal requirements, such as GDPR compliance, and is optimized for search engines.

In conclusion, building an e-commerce website from scratch requires some effort but is achievable with the right tools and resources. With an e-commerce website, you can reach more customers, increase your revenue, and grow your business.

CHOOSING THE PERFECT E-COMMERCE PLATFORM

When it comes to setting up an e-commerce business, one of the most important decisions you will make is choosing the right e-commerce platform. While there are many options available, not all e-commerce platforms are created equal. Your choice of platform will determine the kind of features and tools you have at your disposal, as well as the amount of control you have over your online store.

To choose the perfect e-commerce platform for your business, consider the following factors:

1. Ease of use - The platform should be user-friendly and intuitive, allowing you to easily upload products, manage inventory, and process orders.

2. Customization options - You should be able to customize the look and feel of your e-commerce store to match your brand and stand out from the competition.

3. Payment and shipping integrations - Look for a platform that integrates with all the major payment gateways and offers easy shipping options to help streamline your sales process.

4. Security - Your customers' data must be kept secure and protected from hackers and online threats. Make sure the platform offers robust security features like SSL certificates and regular security updates.

5. Scalability - The platform should be able to grow alongside your business, accommodating more products, features, and users as your business expands.

6. Customer support - A reliable e-commerce platform should offer 24/7 customer support to help you resolve any issues that may arise.

Some popular e-commerce platforms that tick off all these boxes include Shopify, Magento, WooCommerce, and BigCommerce. Each of these platforms has its unique features, pricing, and level of sophistication. Therefore, consider your specific needs, budget, and vision for your e-commerce business before making a decision.

In conclusion, choosing the perfect e-commerce platform for your online store is a critical decision that can determine the success of your business. Look for a platform that offers customization, security, scalability, and customer support, and you're sure to find a platform that is perfect for your needs.

INTEGRATING PAYMENT GATEWAYS AND DIGITAL WALLETS

In today's world, more and more people are opting for online shopping rather than visiting physical stores. Therefore, E-Commerce businesses have become increasingly popular, and to succeed in this market, it is essential to have a reliable payment gateway that can handle online transactions securely and conveniently. Payment gateways are tools that authorize electronic payments by allowing customers to pay for their online purchases using their credit or debit cards, and digital wallets.

It's important to choose a payment gateway that is user-friendly, affordable, and secure. Some of the popular payment gateways are PayPal, Stripe, Square, and Authorize.Net among others. These payment gateways securely store users' card details, making it easier for them to purchase items online without having to enter their card credentials again and again. Also, they provide multiple options for payment methods, including debit cards, credit cards, and digital wallets.

Digital wallets have increasingly become popular as a payment option for E-Commerce transactions. These wallets allow customers to store and easily access their payment information online. They link the customers' credit or debit card information to an app on their phone or computer, making the payment process quick and easy. Examples of popular digital wallets include Google Pay, Apple Pay, and Amazon Pay.

Integrating payment gateways and digital wallets into your E-Commerce website can be a complex task, and it is essential to ensure seamless and secure transactions. It's vital to choose a payment gateway that meets the specific needs of your E-Commerce website. Integration may require technical expertise, so it's highly recommended to work with a professional E-Commerce web developer to integrate payment gateways and digital wallets into your site successfully.

It's equally essential to ensure that the payment gateway is compliant with payment card industry data security standards (PCI DSS). These standards ensure that your customers' payment card data is stored, processed, and transmitted securely. Not complying with these standards may result in significant damages and loss of customer trust.

In a nutshell, integrating payment gateways and digital wallets is crucial to the success of an E-Commerce business. Offering a simple and secure payment process will encourage trust and confidence amongst customers, which will, in turn, lead to increased sales and profitability. Choosing a reliable payment gateway and working with experienced web developers to successfully integrate it into your site will guarantee a seamless and secure payment experience for your customers.

BOOSTING CUSTOMER RETENTION BY OFFERING DISCOUNTS AND PROMOTIONS

One of the biggest challenges that e-commerce businesses face is retaining their customers. With so many options available to consumers, it's important to keep your customers engaged and coming back for more. Offering discounts and promotions is a highly effective way to do just that.

Here are some tips for using discounts and promotions to boost customer retention:

1. Identify your target audience: Before crafting any discounts or promotions, it's important to identify your target audience. Who are your core customers? What are their needs and preferences? Understanding your target audience will help you craft promotions that are highly relevant to them.

2. Offer exclusive promotions: People love feeling like they're part of an exclusive group. Consider offering exclusive promotions to your most loyal customers. For example, you could send out an email with a discount code that only your top customers can use. This is a great way to make your customers feel valued and appreciated.

3. Use urgency and scarcity to drive action: Urgency and scarcity are both powerful motivators. Consider running promotions with limited time frames or limited stock. This can create a sense of urgency and encourage customers to take action quickly.

4. Personalize the experience: Personalization is another powerful way to increase customer loyalty. Consider sending

out personalized promotions based on previous purchases or browsing history. For example, if a customer has been looking at a particular product, you could send them a promotion for that product or a related item.

5. Leverage social media: Social media is a great way to reach new customers and keep existing ones engaged. Consider offering social media exclusive promotions or running contests on your social media channels. This can help increase engagement and drive loyalty.

6. Offer rewards programs: Rewards programs can be highly effective for driving customer retention. Consider offering customers rewards points for each purchase they make. These points can then be redeemed for discounts or other perks. This can help create a sense of loyalty and encourage customers to continue shopping with you.

By following these tips, you can use discounts and promotions to boost customer retention and keep your e-commerce business thriving. Remember, it's not just about acquiring new customers; it's about keeping the ones you have happy and engaged.

ADVANCED E-COMMERCE MARKETING STRATEGIES

In today's digital age, it is not enough to just create an online store and hope that customers will come flocking. With the ever-increasing competition in the E-Commerce industry, it is crucial to implement advanced marketing strategies to stay ahead of the game. Here are some advanced E-Commerce marketing strategies that can help boost your online sales:

1. Personalization: Personalization involves tailoring the experience of each customer according to their preferences and behavior. This requires collecting data about your customers and using it to offer personalized recommendations or promotions. Amazon's "Customers who bought this also bought" is an excellent example of personalization.

2. Artificial Intelligence: The use of AI can help E-Commerce businesses enhance their customer experience. AI can be used to analyze customer data to provide product recommendations, chatbots for customer service, and even visualize customer journeys. This can increase customer satisfaction, reduce churn, and boost sales.

3. Influencer Marketing: Influencer marketing is gaining popularity in the E-Commerce industry as social media platforms continue to grow. Finding the right influencer who has a genuine interest in your product and a significant following can lead to increased visibility and credibility for your brand.

4. Retargeting: Retargeting is the process of targeting customers who have already visited your website but did not make a purchase. Retargeting campaigns are usually done through social

media platforms, where ads can be displayed to customers who have shown an interest in your product or service.

5. User-generated Content: User-generated content (UGC) refers to content created by customers rather than the business itself. UGC includes customer reviews, social media posts, and unboxing videos. Encouraging UGC can help build trust with potential customers, increase brand loyalty, and boost sales.

6. Subscription Services: Subscription services have grown in popularity in recent years. Offering subscriptions can lead to predictable recurring revenue, customer loyalty, and reduce the risk of churn. Subscriptions can also lead to higher average order values as customers tend to purchase more when subscribed.

7. Voice Search Optimization: With the rise of voice search assistants such as Siri, Alexa, and Google Assistant, optimizing your online store for voice search is becoming increasingly important. Voice search optimization involves making your website easier to find through voice search and ensuring your product pages can be easily read aloud.

Implementing these advanced E-Commerce marketing strategies can help you stay competitive in the fast-paced world of online retail. Every E-Commerce business is unique, and it is important to experiment with different marketing strategies to find what works best for your business.

LEVERAGING SOCIAL MEDIA FOR E-COMMERCE SALES

Social media has become an integral part of our daily lives, with billions of people around the world using it to connect, share, and discover content. It is also a powerful tool for businesses to engage with their audience and promote their products or services. In the world of E-Commerce, leveraging social media for sales can be a game-changer. Here are some ways to do it effectively:

1. Understand your audience

The first step to leveraging social media for E-Commerce sales is to understand your audience. You need to know what platforms they use, what type of content they engage with, and what their interests and preferences are. This will help you tailor your social media strategy to reach them effectively.

2. Create engaging content

To stand out on social media, you need to create content that is engaging, visually appealing, and shareable. This can be in the form of images, videos, blog posts, or social media posts. Use high-quality visuals and messaging that resonates with your audience.

3. Use social media advertising

Social media advertising is a cost-effective way to reach your target audience and drive sales. Platforms like Facebook and Instagram offer precise targeting options based on demographics, interests, and behavior. You can also retarget your website visitors or email subscribers to remind them of your products or promotions.

4. Collaborate with influencers

Influencer marketing is a popular trend in E-Commerce, and for a good reason. Influencers have built a loyal following on social media, and partnering with them can increase your brand awareness and credibility. Look for influencers that share your values and have a similar target audience.

5. Offer exclusive promotions

To incentivize your social media followers to make a purchase, create exclusive promotions, such as discounts or free shipping. Make sure to promote them on your social media channels and track their performance.

6. Provide excellent customer service

Social media is a two-way street, and your customers may reach out to you for support or feedback. Make sure to respond promptly and professionally to any inquiries and resolve any issues that arise. Providing excellent customer service can lead to positive reviews and increased customer loyalty.

In conclusion, social media can be a powerful tool for driving sales and building brand awareness in the world of E-Commerce. By understanding your audience, creating engaging content, and leveraging social media advertising and influencer partnerships, you can increase your online presence and boost your bottom line.

UNDERSTANDING CUSTOMER BEHAVIOR THROUGH DATA ANALYTICS

In the world of e-commerce, understanding customer behavior through data analytics is crucial for the success of any business. E-commerce businesses constantly gather data on customer behavior, from browsing patterns to purchasing history, to help identify potential customers and enhance the customer experience. With the right tools and techniques, businesses can gain deep insights into their customer base, enabling them to make informed decisions that drive growth and revenue.

One of the key advantages of e-commerce is the ability to track customer interactions across multiple channels, allowing businesses to gain a more complete view of their customers. For example, by analyzing data from social media platforms, businesses can gain insights into customer preferences and purchasing habits. This can help businesses tailor advertising campaigns to specific segments of their audience, leading to increased engagement and better conversions.

Another important aspect of data analytics in e-commerce is the ability to track website behavior. By analyzing website analytics data, businesses can gain insights into customer browsing patterns, including which pages are most popular, which products are frequently viewed, and which ones are abandoned in the shopping cart. This information can help businesses optimize their website and product offerings to better meet the needs of their customers.

One of the most powerful tools for understanding customer

behavior in e-commerce is customer relationship management (CRM) software. CRM software allows businesses to track customer interactions across multiple touchpoints, facilitating a more holistic view of the customer journey. With this information, businesses can identify customer pain points and find ways to improve the overall customer experience.

Predictive analytics is another important tool in e-commerce customer behavior analysis. Predictive analytics can help businesses identify potential customers based on their digital footprints, leading to more targeted marketing and improved conversion rates. By analyzing past purchasing behavior, businesses can also predict which customers are likely to make future purchases, allowing them to tailor their marketing efforts accordingly.

In conclusion, understanding customer behavior through data analytics is critical in the world of e-commerce. With the right tools and techniques, businesses can gain deep insights into customer preferences and behavior, leading to more effective marketing, better customer engagement, and increased revenue. By investing in data analytics, e-commerce businesses can gain a competitive advantage by building strong, lasting relationships with their customers.

COMMUNICATING EFFECTIVELY WITH CUSTOMERS THROUGH EMAIL AND CHAT SUPPORT

Effective communication is a critical aspect of any business. For E-commerce businesses, communication with customers through email and chat support is an important aspect of building a strong relationship with customers. In today's digital era, customers expect easy communication and fast responses from businesses. Therefore, it's crucial to implement the right strategies to communicate effectively with customers through email and chat support.

One of the most important things to keep in mind is the tone of the communication. Customers appreciate a polite and friendly tone that makes them feel valued, respected and heard. Responding promptly to their inquiries, concerns, and complaints is also important as it showcases a business's dedication towards customer satisfaction.

Using simple and easy-to-understand language is also key to effective communication. As much as possible, avoid using technical terms and acronyms that customers might not be familiar with. Clearly explaining the issue or query and providing well-articulated solutions should be prioritized.

Another important aspect of effective communication is being attentive to the customer's needs. Businesses should try to understand the customer's perspective and empathize with their situation. Being empathetic helps the customer feel heard and valued, and it can turn a potentially negative experience into a positive one.

In addition to email, chat support provides another option to communicate with customers in real-time. Having a live chat option on a business's website can be an effective way to answer customers' questions, and quickly resolve issues. This interactive feature helps businesses build a relationship with customers and provides a platform for any issues or problems to be addressed immediately.

To make things even more effective, having a sound knowledge of the products and services being offered is of utmost importance. This knowledge enables support staff to provide prompt, accurate answers and helps to boost customer confidence in the business.

In conclusion, effective communication with customers is a vital aspect of any E-commerce business. By implementing the right strategies, such as showing empathy, using an appropriate tone of voice, and simplifying language, businesses can build trust, loyalty, and increase customer satisfaction.

HANDLING PRODUCT RETURNS AND REFUNDS FOR YOUR E-COMMERCE BUSINESS

In an E-Commerce business, it is crucial to have a clear and effective returns and refund policy. With the absence of physical stores, customers may be hesitant to purchase products if they are not certain about the return policies. However, providing easy, prompt, and hassle-free returns and refunds can result in increased customer satisfaction and loyalty. Here are some helpful tips for handling product returns and refunds for your E-Commerce business:

1. Create a clear and transparent policy
Make sure your return and refund policy is easy to understand, transparent, and easily accessible. Include details on how customers can return their products, including the address and the expected timeline for the return. Also, specify the conditions for product returns, such as the time frame, the state of the product, and whether the returns are free or chargeable.

2. Implement a user-friendly returns system
To make the returns process smooth and efficient, set up a user-friendly system that allows customers to initiate and track their returns easily. Provide clear instructions on how to initiate the returns and keep them updated on the status of their returns.

3. Offer free returns
Offering free product returns is a great way to encourage customers to buy from your E-Commerce store. Free returns give customers peace of mind when making a purchase and can also establish trust and loyalty.

4. Inspect the returned items quickly

Once you receive returned items, inspect them immediately to ensure they are in good condition, well-packaged, and complete with all the accessories. If they are not, contact the customer and provide a valid justification for the rejection.

5. Refund the payment quickly

After inspecting the returned product and ensuring that everything is in order, proceed with the refund process immediately. It is recommended that you initiate the refund within two business days of receiving the returned item. Consider offering the customer different refund options such as returning the money to their original payment method or issuing a store credit.

6. Use advanced software tools

E-Commerce businesses can use software tools like inventory management software to handle product returns and refunds easily. Such software can track returned products, adjust inventory levels, and automatically process refunds.

In conclusion, handling returns and refunds in your E-Commerce business requires careful planning and execution. By creating clear policies and efficient systems, you can minimize the hassle for your customers and establish long-term trust and loyalty.

ENHANCING THE CUSTOMER EXPERIENCE THROUGH PERSONALIZATION

Personalization has become an increasingly important aspect of E-Commerce in recent years. It refers to tailoring a customer's experience to their specific interests, preferences, and behavior. The objective of personalization is to create a more personalized experience that can attract and retain customers, enhance the customer experience, and ultimately increase sales.

Here are some key ways in which personalization can be used to enhance the customer experience and boost sales:

1. Creating personalized product recommendations: Personalization algorithms can analyze a customer's purchasing history, search history, and other data to recommend products that are likely to be of interest to them. This can not only help a customer find products they are interested in, but it can also increase the chances of a sale.

2. Customizing the user interface: Personalization can also be used to create a customized user interface for each individual customer. By analyzing a customer's browsing patterns and preferences, the E-Commerce website can provide a custom interface that makes it easier for the customer to find the products they want.

3. Offering personalized content: Personalization can also be used to offer personalized content, such as blog posts, videos, and product descriptions, that is tailored to a customer's interests and preferences. This can help to build engagement and loyalty, and ultimately drive sales.

4. Providing personalized recommendations based on location: If an E-Commerce business has multiple physical locations, personalization can be used to offer personalized recommendations based on a customer's location. For example, if a customer is searching for a product on a mobile device while in a particular city, the E-Commerce website could offer recommendations for products that are popular or available in that city.

5. Using personalized email marketing: Personalization can also be used to enhance email marketing campaigns. By analyzing a customer's behavior and preferences, E-Commerce businesses can create customized email campaigns that are more likely to be opened and clicked on.

Conclusion

By using personalization, E-Commerce businesses can provide a more tailored, customized experience to each individual customer. This can enhance the customer experience, increase engagement and loyalty, and ultimately drive sales. Personalization is a powerful tool for businesses looking to stand out in the crowded world of E-Commerce, and it's a trend that is only set to grow in the years ahead.

SCALING UP YOUR E-COMMERCE BUSINESS FOR BIGGER PROFITS

Scaling up an e-commerce business can seem like a daunting task, but it is essential for sustainable growth and bigger profits. Here are some key strategies to help your e-commerce business scale up effectively:

1. Streamline Your Business Processes

As your business grows, it is important to streamline your business processes to ensure that everything runs smoothly. This includes automating repetitive tasks, hiring staff to manage operations, and adopting new technologies to streamline your business.

2. Expand Product Lines

Expanding your product lines can help you tap into new markets and drive more revenue. Consider adding complementary products or creating new products based on customer feedback and demand.

3. Optimize Your Website

Your e-commerce website is your most important asset, so it is essential to optimize it for conversions. This can include improving user experience, optimizing content for search engines, and adding social proof elements such as customer reviews.

4. Optimize Your Supply Chain and Fulfillment

Ensuring that you have the right systems and processes in

place for inventory management, order fulfillment, and shipping is key to scaling up an e-commerce business. This can include outsourcing logistics and fulfillment to a third-party provider, or investing in new systems to automate these processes.

5. Embrace Omni-Channel Selling

Expanding your sales channels beyond your e-commerce store can help you reach new customers and increase revenue. This can include selling on marketplaces such as Amazon or eBay, adding social selling features, and even opening a brick-and-mortar store.

6. Focus on Customer Retention

Customer retention is critical for long-term growth and profitability. Implementing customer loyalty programs, offering personalized experiences, and providing exceptional customer service can help keep customers coming back and driving more revenue.

7. Invest in Marketing and Advertising

Investing in marketing and advertising can help drive more traffic and sales to your e-commerce store. This can include paid advertising such as Google Ads or Facebook Ads, influencer marketing, and content marketing.

In Conclusion

Scaling up an e-commerce business requires a combination of strategic planning, dedication, and hard work. Focusing on key areas such as streamlining business processes, expanding product lines, optimizing your website, optimizing your supply chain and fulfillment, embracing omni-channel selling, focusing on customer retention, and investing in marketing and advertising can help set your e-commerce business on the path to bigger profits and sustainable growth.

MASTERING THE ART OF DROPSHIPPING

As an E-Commerce business owner, you want to provide your customers with reliable products that they can cherish. However, there are a number of challenges that come with managing a product inventory. For example, holding onto an excessive amount of stock may lead to cash flow problems. One strategy that can help avoid these challenges while still thriving in the world of E-Commerce is called dropshipping.

Dropshipping is a way to run your online shop without having to keep an inventory. Essentially, when a customer orders a product on your website, you contact a third-party vendor who ships the product directly to the customer. This means that you don't have to pay for the product until it sells, and you don't need to worry about storing it or shipping it yourself.

Here are a few tips on how to master the art of dropshipping:

1. Find the right supplier: The first step to mastering dropshipping is to find a supplier who offers high-quality products, has reasonable prices, and is reliable in shipping the products. Research your options and read reviews to make sure you are working with trustworthy suppliers.

2. Set fair prices: Pricing is key when it comes to E-Commerce. While dropshipping can help you save money on not having inventory, it is still essential to price your products appropriately. Consider the cost of the product and any fees you may be charged by the supplier, and be sure to factor shipping costs into your pricing strategy.

3. Optimize your website: Make your website user-friendly and

easy to navigate. Your website should have clear and concise product descriptions, high-quality images, and an easy-to-use shopping cart. With dropshipping, the supplier will typically take care of shipping and returns for your customers. Make sure your website also has a clear customer service policy and clear contact information.

4. Focus on customer service: Providing excellent customer service is important in any E-Commerce business, and it is especially important when dropshipping, as you rely on vendors for timely shipping and accurate product descriptions. Consider offering a customer service guarantee, such as a friendly return policy and fast delivery.

5. Optimize your business operations: It is important to automate as much of the dropshipping process as possible, such as keeping track of inventory, processing orders promptly, and quickly resolving any customer service issues. Automating these tasks will help you focus on growing your business and driving more sales.

Dropshipping can be an excellent strategy for E-Commerce businesses looking to expand without the added expenses of inventory management. Using the tips above, begin the process of mastering the art of dropshipping to help your business thrive.

FINDING THE RIGHT SUPPLIERS AND NEGOTIATING DEALS TO EXPAND YOUR PRODUCT LINE

In the world of e-commerce, having a wide range of products and a constantly updated inventory is crucial in attracting and retaining customers on your site. But as your business grows and your customer base expands, the daunting task of sourcing and negotiating deals with multiple suppliers can become overwhelming. This is where having the right suppliers can make all the difference in the success of your e-commerce business.

The following are some tips for finding the best suppliers for your business:

1. Do Your Research: Finding and selecting quality suppliers requires a thorough research process. You should evaluate the reliability, quality, and pricing of potential suppliers before committing to a deal. Look for reviews, ratings, and testimonials from other e-commerce entrepreneurs to gauge the supplier's reputation and track record in the industry.

2. Attend Trade Shows: Attending trade shows is another way to find potential suppliers. Trade shows can provide you with access to a wide range of suppliers in one location, and it allows for a chance to network with other participants in the industry. This is also the perfect opportunity to see the latest products and trends in the market.

3. Use Online Directories: Online supplier directories like Alibaba, Oberlo, and Salehoo can serve as a starting point in your search for potential suppliers. These directories offer a wide range of suppliers from different niches and industries, making it easier

for you to find the right supplier for your business.

4. Negotiate the Best Deal: Once you have identified potential suppliers, the next step is to negotiate the best deal. Keep in mind that pricing is just one component of a good deal. You need to consider other factors such as shipping terms, delivery timelines, product warranties, and return policies.

5. Build Strong Relationships: Building strong relationships with your suppliers is critical to the long-term success of your e-commerce business. Regular communication, consistent payments, and prompt feedback can help foster a strong working relationship, leading to better deals and preferred terms.

In conclusion, finding the right suppliers and negotiating great deals is a continuous process in building a successful e-commerce business. By conducting thorough research, attending trade shows, using online directories, negotiating the best deal, building strong relationships, and staying up-to-date with industry changes and trends, you'll be well on your way to expanding your product line and keeping your customers happy.

STAYING AHEAD OF THE COMPETITION WITH INNOVATIVE E-COMMERCE STRATEGIES

In today's highly competitive E-Commerce market, standing out from the crowd is crucial in order to attract and retain customers. This requires the implementation of innovative strategies that can keep your E-Commerce business ahead of its competition. In this chapter, we will discuss some of the cutting-edge E-Commerce strategies that successful businesses are using today to stay ahead of the curve.

1. Subscription Services:

Subscription services have been gaining popularity in recent years, giving users access to exclusive content or products on a regular basis. This strategy is highly successful in industries like fashion, beauty, and entertainment, where customers are always searching for the newest and latest products.

2. Voice Search Optimization:

The rise of voice assistants such as Amazon's Alexa and Google Home has made voice search one of the fastest-growing segments in SEO. Voice search optimization involves targeting long-tail keywords and adding more conversational phrases into your website's content to appeal to customers using voice search.

3. Influencer Marketing:

Influencer marketing is a highly effective way of promoting products and services to a large and highly targeted audience.

By partnering with social media influencers who have a large following, E-Commerce businesses can tap into the trust and loyalty of their audience and drive sales.

4. Augmented Reality:

Augmented reality is a technology that superimposes 3D graphics onto the real-world environment, allowing customers to experience products in a more interactive way. This is highly popular in the furniture and clothing industries, where customers can visualize products in their homes or try on clothes virtually.

5. Personalization:

In today's highly competitive E-Commerce market, personalization will set your business apart. By recommending products and offering personalized suggestions during the purchasing process, E-Commerce businesses can create a more unique and personalized shopping experience for their customers, which can lead to brand loyalty.

6. Social Commerce:

Social commerce involves the integration of social media platforms directly into the E-Commerce experience. By allowing customers to make purchases without leaving the social media platform, businesses can capitalize on the large and highly active follower bases of these platforms.

In conclusion, there's a lot that E-Commerce businesses can do to stay ahead of the curve. By implementing innovative strategies such as those outlined above, businesses can set themselves apart from the rest of the pack and attract more customers.

CONCLUSION: FUTURE PREDICTIONS FOR E-COMMERCE AND ITS IMPACT ON THE BUSINESS WORLD

As the world becomes increasingly digital, E-Commerce is poised to be a major driving force behind the growth of businesses. The convenience and accessibility of online shopping, coupled with the rising trend of mobile purchasing, has only fueled the growth of E-Commerce. As such, businesses that can offer a hassle-free, user-friendly experience to their customers stand to gain a significant competitive advantage.

With technology continually evolving, the future of E-Commerce promises to be exciting. Progressive web apps and artificial intelligence are just some of the technologies that are increasingly being used to offer customers a more personalized and efficient experience. The integration of augmented and virtual reality is also bound to increase online sales by allowing customers to visualize products in more detail and even place them in their own environment.

The influence of social media in E-Commerce sales shows no signs of slowing down, either. Businesses that can leverage social media platforms, like Facebook and Instagram, to reach their target market, will undoubtedly benefit from the trend for years to come. It will be important for E-Commerce businesses to recognize and adapt to the ever-changing trends in digital marketing to succeed in today's fast-paced world.

One major factor that will shape the future of E-Commerce is the increasing focus on sustainability. Consumers are becoming more eco-conscious and expect businesses to take steps to reduce their environmental impact. E-Commerce businesses that prioritize eco-friendliness and ethical sourcing practices can expect to attract a growing customer base.

In conclusion, E-Commerce is a powerful tool that businesses can use to expand their reach and grow their profits. The future of the E-Commerce industry promises to be one of continual innovation, and businesses that can keep up with these changes will undoubtedly thrive. By focusing on delivering an exceptional customer experience, keeping up with technology trends, and incorporating sustainable practices into their business models, E-Commerce businesses can look forward to a bright future.

www.ingramcontent.com/pod-product-compliance
Lightning Source LLC
Chambersburg PA
CBHW071145220526
45467CB00015B/1928